ro.
).
&
Nadal. 110p. Theatre Arts. 1969.
$3.85. LC 69-17967.
THEATER

Comparing three readily accessible translations of this celebrated play, I find Miss Raine's the best for its clarity to the ear and lack of those clichés that mark and mar so many translations, especially from Spanish dramatic literature. Actors and directors interested in translations from Spanish drama, but hitherto defeated by nearly all of those available, will discover this one with relief and admiration. That Raine (in consultation with Nadal, a man of the theater) has made no effort to follow the original metre and rhyme is of benefit to us and to the spirit of Calderón's text.—*James Sandoe, English/Humanities Department, University of Colorado, Boulder*

LIFE'S A DREAM

CALDERON

LIFE'S A DREAM
LA VIDA ES SUENO

A Play in Three Acts

TRANSLATED FROM THE SPANISH BY
KATHLEEN RAINE
AND
R. M. NADAL

THEATRE ARTS BOOKS
NEW YORK

NOTE

THE purpose of this new version of Calderon's most famous play *La Vida es Sueno* is to provide a verse translation actable on the modern stage. For this reason no attempt has been made to reproduce the metre and rhyme of the original. In the rendering of as many meanings as possible of the original poetry, Kathleen Raine (who is responsible for the English version) has at every stage worked in close collaboration with R. M. Nadal, whose knowledge of the Spanish theatre has been her guide.

The original suggestion that the authors should translate this play came from Rupert Doone of the Group Theatre, who was never able to put on the production he planned, but who went so far as to have scenery and costumes designed by Robert Medley. This version is dedicated to the memory of his genius.

R. M. NADAL   KATHLEEN RAINE

CHARACTERS

BASILIO, *King of Poland*
SEGISMUNDO, *Prince of Poland*
ASTOLFO, *Duke of Muscovy*
CLOTALDO, *An old Lord*
PIPER, *Fool, servant to Rosaura*
ROSAURA, *A Lady*
ESTRELLA, *Infanta*

Soldiers, guards, musicians, retainers,
servants, ladies, etc.

ACT ONE

Scene One

On one side a rugged mountain, on the other, a tower, whose ground floor is used as SEGISMUNDO'S *prison. The door facing the audience is ajar. The action begins at nightfall.*

ROSAURA, PIPER.

ROSAURA, *dressed as a man, appears high up on the rocks and climbs down to the plain.*

ROSAURA: Are you the fabulous hippogriff running in
        harness with the wind?
    Flameless thunderbolt, featherless bird, fish
        without scales,
    Monster of the four elements without instinct
        to check your headlong flight?
    Where are you heading for, runaway horse
    Bolting into the barren labyrinth of these rocks
    Until your wild impulse plunges you down
        some precipice?
    Go, then; stray on this mountain-side
    Where the unbroken colts wait for their
        Phaethon!
    For I must go on; in the dark, in despair,
    With no path to follow but the way that lies
        before my feet,
    Down the rough entangled wilderness of this
        mountain
    Whose great brow now is frowning at the sun.

I

An unkind welcome, Poland, you give the
    stranger,
For at your frontier you demand his signature
    in blood:
His troubles await him on arrival; that is plain.
My own case proves it; but in what country
Did a luckless creature ever find pity?

PIPER: Two luckless creatures, you should say, not
    one;
Two of us, the more fools we,
Set out from home to seek our fortunes,
And now not one of us, but two
Thanks to folly and bad luck
Have come tumbling down this scree—
I have had my troubles as well as you,
So don't leave me out when you complain!

ROSAURA: Poor Piper! Don't imagine
That I want to lay claim to all our woes!
I assumed, of course,
That you would rather bewail your own.
I won't deprive you of the satisfaction of
    grumbling!
And one philosopher says that telling our
    troubles is such a pleasure
That a wise man should always court disaster.

PIPER: That philosopher of yours, in my opinion,
Was drunk. Ha! Wouldn't I like to slap his
    face
To give him something to cry for!
The harder the slap, the better the story!
But, madam, what about us? Here we are,
Lost, on foot, night coming on,
In an uninhabited wilderness!
Somewhere the sun is shining, I dare say,
But here it's setting!

2

ROSAURA: A sad plight, certainly;
But unless my fancy is deceiving me, I see a
    building
Lit by the last ominous beams which still hold
    back the day.

PIPER: I see it too—unless it's my wishful thinking!

ROSAURA: Among these barren crags, so rude and mean
    a tower
It seems to cower in shadow, hiding from the
    sun;
Built of blocks so roughly hewn
Among the fallen stones, ablaze in the last
    fire of day,
It looks like some gigantic boulder
Tumbled from the mountain's shoulder.

PIPER: Very well, let's go—what are we waiting for?
I see no point, madam, in admiring the view
When there is a chance that whoever lives
    down there
May give us bed and supper—

ROSAURA: The door—or should I say the mournful
    mouth—is open.
From it the night is born,
For there, within, it is begotten . . .

PIPER: Ooer! What's that noise?

ROSAURA: I cannot move hand or foot—
I'm hot and cold at once!

PIPER: Chains! Chains clinking!
It's a galley-slave's ghost!
I'm so frightened, it must be that!

SEGISMUNDO: Misery! Oh, misery! Most wretched o
men!

ROSAURA: What sorrowing voice was that?
Am I to find
Only more grief and suffering here?

PIPER: I only find more fear!

ROSAURA: Piper!

PIPER: Yes, my lady?

ROSAURA: Let us get away from the danger of thi
haunted tower!

PIPER: My knees are too weak to run, if it comes t
that!

ROSAURA: Look—that spent flash, like a wan star
flickering and trembling
Is it a lamp? Do you see—throbbing
Like a dying pulse, glimmering in the gloom
seeming
Only to darken the darkness—yes, it is—
And I can just make out the interior of a
prison-cell,
Grave of the living dead!
And look—a man dressed in the skin of some
wild animal,
Loaded with chains, only a lamp for company!
We cannot get away,
So let us listen to what he is saying,
And learn what his sorrows may be.

4

SEGISMUNDO: Misery! Oh, misery! Most wretched of men!
The punishment is plain—
Nor do I question your stern justice, Heaven,
But what my crime is I have yet to learn.
Indeed Man's original sin is to be born,
But, Heaven, beyond that common crime of
birth,
Tell me—for I shall never sleep at nights until
I know
In what else have I offended you?
Are not other men born too?
Why must I suffer more than other sons of
earth?
The bird is born; clothed in beauty, a feathered
flower,
A winged nosegay, it rises into the air
Abandoning its nest, to soar
High up, with never a care:
Must I, whose soul aspires, be less free?

The wild beast is born—its spotted skin
Painted in rivalry of the zodiac of heaven,
And yet how cruel in its struggle to survive,
Each beast a monster of its own labyrinth:
And I, less cruel by instinct, must I be less free?

The fish is born; it draws no breath of life,
Spawned among weeds and slime, a ship of
scales
This way and that it drifts, mirrored by the
waves,
Measuring the cold distances of the sea's
expanse:
Must I, endowed with free will, be less free?

The brook is born, a silver snake, sinuous
Among the flowers it uncoils, ripples and sings

5

As the wide blossoming kingdom of th
    fields
Unfolds on either side; it flows to the sea;
And I, a living being, must I be less free?

Oh God who has bestowed on brook, fish
    beast and bird
So sweet a gift,
What justice, law or reason can withhold
From man all nature's privilege and joy?
Etna's imprisoned fires rage in me,
And I could tear out of my breast
The burning fragments of my heart!

ROSAURA: His lament fills me with pity and terror!

SEGISMUNDO: Who has overheard me? Is it Clotaldo?

PIPER: Say yes!

ROSAURA: Only another sorrower who in these col
    vaults has heard your lament.

SEGISMUNDO: Then I will kill you!
For you have witnessed what no-one mus
    know, my weakness—
I will tear you to pieces just for that—and m
    hands are not weak—

PIPER: I am deaf—I didn't hear a word you said!

ROSAURA: Mercy! If you are human, spare me—
I kneel at your feet!

SEGISMUNDO: How your voice moves me!
Your looks amaze me!
Your pleading touches me—
Tell me who you are!—
Although I know so little of the world
(For this tower has been to me both cradl
    and grave)
Although since I was born
(If this living death may be called birth)

6

I have seen nothing of the world beyond this
    mountain
Where I die my life, or live my death;
Although I have not seen or spoken with
Any but the one man who knows my mis-
    fortune,
Thanks to him I know something of earth and
    heaven—
Yes, I could astonish you—
You may still call me human,
A human monster, man among beasts, beast
    among men.

And what is more, I have studied natural law,
Learned it from the animals and the birds,
And measured the revolutions of the peaceful
    stars:

Yet you, and you alone
Have ever checked my anger,
Astonished my eyes, made me hang upon your
    words.

Each time I look at you, I am filled with
    wonder—
The more I look, the more desire
To look and wonder more and more.
There is a fever in my eyes;
Drinking means death, and yet I die to gaze.
Let me look at you, and die!
Yes, if to look at you is to die, I surrender—
For not to see you would be worse than death,
It would be furious, raging, bitter pain of
    death in life!
This is a paradox of life and death:
By granting a sorrower his life
It seems that I must die of joy, or live in grief.

ROSAURA: I am so amazed by your appeareance,
So astonished at your story,
I scarcely know what to ask you, or what to
reply;
Except that Heaven must have brought me
here today for my comfort,
If comfort it may be called
For one sorrower to see another yet more
unfortunate.
There was once a learned man, so I have heard,
so poor
That he lived only on the herbs he gathered
'Could there be anyone poorer and worse off
than I am?' he wondered:
Then he looked back, and saw the answer:
another scholar
Was gathering up the leaves he threw away.
And so I have travelled through the world
complaining:
And when I asked if anyone could be more
unhappy,
You gave me a merciful answer; now I see
That my sorrows you would have welcomed
as happiness.
So, if my troubles can in any way lighten
yours,
Listen carefully; you are welcome to those I
am about to let fall.
My name is . . .

Scene Three

CLOTALDO:	Guards of the tower!
	Are you asleep, or neglecting your duty? Two men
	Have broken in.
ROSAURA:	Here comes more trouble.
SEGISMUNDO:	This is Clotaldo, guardian of my prison;
	So my misfortunes are not ended!
CLOTALDO:	Don't give them time to defend themselves,
	Arrest them instantly, or kill them!
VOICES (*off*):	Treason, etc.
PIPER:	Guards of the tower
	Who let us come in,
	If there's a choice
	We would much prefer
	Instant arrest
	To being killed!

(CLOTALDO *and* SOLDIERS *appear, all masked;* CLOTALDO *carries a pistol*)

CLOTALDO:	Mask your faces! While we are here
	No-one must know who we are
PIPER:	Oho! A masquerade!
CLOTALDO:	Fools, whoever you are who have trespassed here
	Against the king's decree that no intruder
	May enter this forbidden ground
	Or spy into the secret of this rocky solitude
	Your arms and lives you must surrender
	Before this metal serpent spits its venom
	And the crack of two bullets splits the air.
SEGISMUNDO:	Tyrant master! Before you touch a hair of their heads
	I will slough off my life along with these miserable shackles,

9

	I will destroy myself in spite of them,
	With my hands, with my teeth, against these rocks
	Rather than see them ill-treated.
CLOTALDO:	You died before you were born, Segismundo!
	And Providence has decreed this prison, as you know well
	As a curb, a wheel to check your violence!
	So why do you boast? (*to* GUARDS) Shut the door of the gaol,
	Keep him inside, out of the way!
SEGISMUNDO:	You Heavens!
	You are right to rob me of my liberty!
	For, if I were free, I would be that Titan
	Who to shatter the crystal mirrors of the sun
	Piled the jade mountains on their stone foundations!
CLOTALDO:	And is it not to prevent the violence you plan
	That you have to suffer now so many pains?

ROSAURA: Sir, if such pride offend you,
It seems best to plead humbly
For a life that is in your hands;
Perhaps you will be moved to pity,
For surely you cannot be so stern
That neither humility nor pride can bend
you?

PIPER: And if neither Pride nor Humility,
Two characters to whom thousands of
Morality Plays
Owe their popularity,
Can influence you, then I,
Who am neither proud nor humble but fifty-
fifty
Beg you not to be too hard on us!

CLOTALDO: You, there!

SOLDIERS: Yes, Sir!

CLOTALDO: Disarm them both; blindfold them.
They must not see how or from whence they
go.

ROSAURA: This sword of mine I will surrender
Only to yourself, since here you are in
command;
My sword yields only to the noblest.

PIPER: Mine doesn't care who takes it,
Has not the least objection
To the lowest of the low; (*to* GUARD) here,
you can have it!

ROSAURA: And if I must die, in pledge of this
courtesy
I leave you a weapon once highly prized
By the gentleman who wore it; I beg you to
keep it;

11

This gold-hilted sword enshrines a mystery.
   I came to Poland
To avenge a wrong.
Trusting in its protection.

CLOTALDO: (*aside*)   (What is this?
Now my worry and perplexity,
My unhappiness and misgivings, are greater
   than ever!)
Who gave you this sword?

ROSAURA: A woman.

CLOTALDO: What was her name?

ROSAURA   That I cannot tell you.

CLOTALDO: Then why do you suppose—or know—
That this sword enshrines a secret?

ROSAURA: The lady who gave it me said, 'Go to
   Poland,
'By one means or another contrive that this
   sword be seen
'By the highest in the land.
'One there, I know, if he should see it
'Will help and protect you.' But his name
She did not tell me, lest he should be dead.

CLOTALDO: Now Heaven come to my aid! Can I have
   heard aright?
Can this be possible, or do I only imagine
This is the sword I left with lovely Violante
As a pledge that whoever should gird it on
   would find in me
A loving son, or tender father!

Now its bearer who comes seeking my
   protection
Has found in me his executioner—
He is condemned already—what can I do?
What a strange, sad, perplexing trick of Fate!

12

This is my son! The beating of my heart
Confirms the evidence of the sword.
My heart knocks under my ribs like a caged
bird,
Beats its wings against the bars and locks it
cannot break
But peers out, like a poor prisoner
Who hears a commotion in the street.
The eyes are the heart's windows, where the
prisoner stands and weeps.
Oh, God, what should I do? What shall I do?
If I hand him over to the King, which is my
duty,
I send him to his death.
To conceal him would be to break my oath of
loyalty.
On the one hand, personal honour, on the
other, public duty!
Both claims are overwhelming; but I must not
weaken—
Loyalty to the King is above life, and there-
fore above honour.
So loyalty must live, and honour die.

Besides—what were his words just now
About a crime against his honour?
A man who has lost his reputation is no son
of mine!
Has none of my blood in his veins, for my
blood is noble!
No, not my son!
                    But after all, it is possible—
For honour is so delicate, such fragile stuff
That one rash act can break it, a breath stain
it—

That he suffered some quite unavoidable
  affront—
Then what more could he do, as a man of
  honour, what more, after all,
Than travel here, at so much risk, to clear his
  name?
He is my son! My blood is in him, for he has
  courage!
The best course is to go to the King:
I will tell him that this man under sentence of
  death is my son.
Perhaps out of regard for my honour, the
  King will pardon him;
And if I merit his life, I will help him recover
  his good name.
But if the King will not remit his sentence,
Then he shall die without knowing I am his
  father.

(*to* ROSAURA *and* PIPER)

Come with me, strangers;
Don't imagine you are alone in your mis-
  fortunes!
On this balance
Where all of us are hanging in suspense
Who can say whether life or death would be
  the worse misfortune?

Scene Five

A Court Room in the Royal Palace. Enter, on one side,
ASTOLFO *with* ATTENDANT SOLDIERS; *on the other side,*
INFANTA ESTRELLA, *and* LADIES. *Martial music and salvoes*

ASTOLFO: How well those drums and trumpets
    With music of birds and fountains
    Blend their differing salvoes!

    Lady, those eyes so dazzle
    Nature with rays celestial
    That in confusion all
    Astounded, look, the birds
    Amazed, become winged trumpets
    And trumpets birds of brass!

    The guns as Queen salute you,
    Birds as Aurora praise you
    And flowers as Flora greet you.

    You come, bright day eclipsing,
    Joy like Aurora bringing,
    In peace, like Flora coming,
    Pallas in war advancing,
    As Queen, my soul subduing—
ESTRELLA: Speech, Sir, with deeds should tally;
    This martial force belies
    Your words of flattery.

    Worse than a beast the man
    Who comes with flattering tongue
    Planning deceit and treason!
ASTOLFO: You are misinformed, Estrella,
    If you think me insincere,
    Reject my compliments as vain.

Please allow me to explain
My train of thought; when the King of
    Poland—
I mean, Eustorgio the Third,
Died, Basilio was heir apparent,
And, after him, the King's two daughters,
Your and my respective mothers—
I won't tire you with the details—
Your mother, Clorilene, the elder,
Beyond the stars has now her empire,
While the Princess Recisunda—
May long life and health attend her—
That is, your aunt, my honoured mother,
Married in Muscovy, my country.

Now, Madam, do you begin to see?

Basilio is no longer young,
And more inclined to pass his time
In study, than to contemplate
A second marriage; we are his heirs.
You are of the elder line,
But my claim stronger, being a man,
And likely, therefore, to be preferred.
Our uncle knows the circumstances,
And, in fact, has summoned us
To settle our disputed claims
In this very day and place.
And I, for that sole purpose
In peace have come from Muscovy
To find that you with beauty armed make war
    on me!
If love, wise love were present here
To plead the popular desire,
By my free will, you should be Queen.
Our Uncle should bestow his crown

On you, to mark a victory
Whose triumph makes my heart your empire!

ESTRELLA: These thoughts of yours are generous;
And I would like to be no less
Magnanimous than yourself, and happy
If the throne were mine, if only
Because I then could make it yours.
Only, my heart has grave misgivings!
Your speeches are belied, I fear
By that miniature you wear!

ASTOLFO: I can perfectly reassure you—
Only there is no time now,
The sound of drums announces the arrival
Of the King, attended by his Council.

(*Enter* KING BASILIO *with* COURTIERS)

Scene Six

ESTRELLA: Sage Thales—

ASTOLFO: Learned Euclid—

ESTRELLA: Who, by the planets

ASTOLFO: Who, by the constellation

ESTRELLA: Today rules

ASTOLFO: Today governs

ESTRELLA: The orbits of planets

ASTOLFO: The paths of the star

ESTRELLA: That you describe,

ASTOLFO: You compute and measure

ESTRELLA: Let me in embraces tender

ASTOLFO: Let me, your humble servitor

ESTRELLA: Be to your oak the ivy slender!

ASTOLFO: At your feet lie in surrender!

BASILIO: Sweet niece, kind nephew—you are mos welcome;

I have sent for you, and you have obeyed my summons

Most loyally—a proof of love.

Believe me, neither of you will have cause fo grievance,

For I intend to make you equals;

And now, when I confess

My years are becoming a burden and a weariness,

I hope you will attend my speech in silence.

What I have to tell you will surprise you;

And therefore, I ask you, my well-loved niece and nephew,

And all of you who are our friends, our kinsmen and our subjects,

18

To listen with strict attention. As all of you
    know well
My scientific studies have earned for me
The epithet by which the whole world knows
    me,
'Basilio the Sage'. The artist's brush and
    sculptor's chisel
Have given me an universal fame
As 'Basilio the Great'. You also know
That I have made my special study the subtle
    mathematics
By whose power I anticipate time, and make
    news stale;
For those events which arrive from day to
    day
Are already present in my tables of the
    coming centuries;
Time is, in fact, indebted to me:
It has only to repeat what I have already
    foretold.
Those concentric spheres, as snow immacu-
    late,
The sky's crystal canopy
That the sun's rays illumine
And the moon traverses,
The diamond orbs and globes,
The star-hung firmament
Where the constellations abide,
Have been my life-long study;
For are not these the books
In whose sapphire volumes,
Upon whose diamond pages
Heaven writes, in golden lines,
In legible characters,
The destinies of men,

For good or ill! And when
I read these sentences
My thought accompanies
The swift heavenly bodies
In their eternal courses.

Would that an outraged Heaven
Had made me its first victim,
For I have paid the price;
A terrible price for my skill
In indexing Heaven's pages,
Writing my marginal comment:
He whose foreknowledge dooms him
Enacts his suicide,
His gifts are knives to wound him;
And so it is with me,
As you will understand
When you have heard my story.
Once more, I crave your silence.

My Queen bore me a son
At whose ill-omened birth
The heavens rained down portents.
While still he was shut away
From the beautiful light of earth
Within the womb entombed
(They are much alike, death and birth)
Many times his mother
In a recurrent nightmare
Saw a human monster
That rent her body open
And came bloodstained into the world
Like a viper—his mother's murderer.
The day of his birth arrived:
The omens were fulfilled
(For, late or soon,

Prophecies are fulfilled
Lest we should call them lies).

At my son's nativity
The blood-red sun had entered
Into fierce opposition
With the moon; earth in shadow
Lay like an arena
For the two great luminaries,
The champions of Heaven,
Unable to come to grips
Did battle with their beams;
Never had eclipse
So aweful overshadowed
The sun, since, weeping blood,
It mourned the death of Christ!
In multitudinous fires
Consumed, the great orb seemed
In throes of dissolution;
Darkness obscured the sky,
Earth quaked, and buildings trembled,
The clouds rained meteorites,
The rivers ran with blood.

In this delirious nightmare
Of the sun, my son was born—
Segismundo; and, as a first
Foretaste of his nature,
Savage, even at his birth,
He murdered his own mother,
As if he would declare,
'Already I am a man,
Rewarding good with evil.'

I retired into my study;
And there, and everywhere

21

Found proof that Segismundo
Would be a man without scruple,
Impious as a king,
And as a prince, cruel.
I foresaw through him the kingdom,
By vice and treachery
Divided, torn
By civil war; foresaw
That, carried away by the fury
Of his rebellion
He would rise up against me—
And—I can scarcely tell it
For shame—I saw myself
Deposed, vanquished, prostrate,
And my white hairs brought low,
Spread at his feet like a carpet.

I believed the omens—
Who would not?—For the student
Shut away in solitude
Is the victim of self-pride.
Placing my faith, therefore
In the signs that foretold disaster
I thought it best to confine
The monster born to me.
'Now I shall see' I thought, 'what power
'A sage has over the stars!'

So it was given out that the child had been
    still-born;
And I built a secret tower up in yonder
    mountain
Among rocks and boulder-stones where not
    even the light can penetrate
Past the rough monoliths which intercept its
    passage.

This is the reason for the law, publicly
    proclaimed,
Forbidding entry to that valley on pain of
    death.
There Segismundo lives, wretched, a poor
    prisoner,
There only Clotaldo has seen him, instructed
    him in religion;
And only Clotaldo knows what he has
    suffered.

Now, I must call your attention
To three contradictory aspects of this
    matter.
First—that I acted from a sense of duty to my
    country;
I wished to safeguard Poland from oppression
    and servitude
Under a tyrant; such was our royal duty.

Second—in depriving my own son
Of rights that are his, by laws both divine and
    human
I would act against Christian charity; no law
    can justify
Tyranny to prevent tyranny; I would be
    guilty of that crime
To prevent my son from being the tyrant I
    myself had been.

Finally, I see that I was wrong to give such
    easy credence
To the foretold events.
Even though his nature might lead him to the
    precipice
He need not fall.

Adverse fate, ill-aspected planets, natural
   violence
Cannot override free-will:
The stars incline us, but they cannot compel.

Having long weighed, therefore, these matters
   in my mind
I have found, after much thought, a solution,
Which may come as a shock to you all; it is
   this:
Tomorrow, without his knowing he is my
   son, or King of Poland,
I will place Prince Segismundo upon my
   throne,
Under our royal canopy; in fact, he shall
   reign,
With full authority, in my place.
All who are here present are to assemble, and
   swear allegiance;
Thus I shall obtain a threefold answer to my
   three questions:
If he prove in every way prudent, and
   virtuous, and wise,
Belieing the auguries, then you shall enjoy
   your rightful prince;
Whose court has been the mountains, the
   beasts his sole companions.
But if, on the contrary, he is proud, cruel and
   insolent,
Giving free rein to the evil in his nature,
Then at least I shall have done my duty:
If I then depose him and send him back to
   prison
I shall have acted from justice, and not from
   cruelty.

24

And if such should be the case, my beloved
    subjects,
I will give you a king and queen more worthy
    of crown and sceptre,
Our nephew and niece,
Their rival claims united in bonds of marriage,
    each shall receive
What each so well deserves.
This is a King's edict, a father's request,
A sage's counsel, an old man's advice;
And if Spanish Seneca says truly that a King
    is nothing
But his country's humble servant, a slave's
    petition!

ASTOLFO: If it falls to me to answer,
As being, of those here present, the most
    directly affected,
In the name of all, I say, let Segismundo be
    brought!

ALL: Long live our Prince!
Long live Segismundo! etc.

BASILIO: Thanks, my subjects, for your loyal support.
Accompany these two pillars of our State
To their apartments; tomorrow you shall see
    him.

ALL: Long live Basilio the Great!

CLOTALDO: Sire, may I speak?

BASILIO: Oh, Clotaldo, I am glad to see you!

CLOTALDO: It is always a joyful privilege to kneel before
                  you,
              But this time, Sire, the tragic occasion
              Proves the exception.

BASILIO: Why so?

CLOTALDO: Sire, I have suffered a misfortune
              In what might have been my greatest joy!

BASILIO: Continue!

CLOTALDO: This handsome boy,
              Perhaps headstrong, perhaps unwittingly,
              Entered the tower, and saw Prince Segis-
                  mundo,
              And this boy is . . .

BASILIO: Do not afflict yourself, Clotaldo.
              Had this occurred on any other day
              I too should have been sorry; but now
              The secret is disclosed, and it no longer
                  matters
              That he should know what I myself have told.
              Come and see me presently; I have much to
                  say,
              And I must warn you, you have a part to play
              In an event whose like the world has never
                  seen!
              As for these two prisoners, do not be anxious,
              They will not be punished for your negli-
                  gence—
              They are pardoned!

CLOTALDO: Sire! May you live a thousand ages!

CLOTALDO:	Heaven came to my assistance!
	I need not now declare he is my son!
ROSAURA:	I have no words to thank you!
PIPER:	Nor have I!
ROSAURA:	I owe my life to you, sir,
	And that life is yours for ever to command—
CLOTALDO:	You owe me nothing!
	A gentleman without honour cannot be said to live,
	And if, as you have told me,
	You have come to Poland to avenge dishonour,
	I have not saved your life!
	A man without honour is as good as dead!
	(Surely that will goad him into speech!)
ROSAURA:	The life I owe you is, I confess, not mine;
	But my revenge shall clear my honour,
	And then my life shall be a gift worth giving!
CLOTALDO:	Take this bright sword of yours!
	I do not doubt your enemy's blood upon it
	Will clear your honour; for my sword
	(That is to say, a sword that has been in my possession,
	So recently, even for so short a time)
	Will know how to avenge its wearer!
ROSAURA:	I gird it on, then, in your name,
	And upon it, I swear vengeance,
	Even though my enemy
	Were ten times greater than he is!
CLOTALDO:	He is powerful, then?
ROSAURA:	So great that I cannot name him;
	I would willingly entrust
	Greater secrets to your discretion,

27

	But if you knew it, you might withdraw your kindness and protection!
CLOTALDO:	On the contrary—if you name him it will prevent me
	From helping your enemy unwittingly.
	(*aside*) I would give a great deal to know who he is!
ROSAURA:	I will—to prove my gratitude I will tell you.
	My enemy is Astolfo, Duke of Muscovy!
CLOTALDO:	(*aside*) (This is certainly worse than I had imagined!
	I must not appear distressed!—But I must know more)
	As a Muscovite subject, you cannot
	Take up a personal quarrel against your sovereign.
	I advise you to go back to Muscovy; try to overcome
	The strain of rashness in your character
	That is heading you towards a precipice—
ROSAURA:	He is my prince, yet he has wronged me!
CLOTALDO:	That is impossible—even if he struck you in the face!
ROSAURA:	His offence was much greater!
CLOTALDO:	Tell me the truth—for you can tell me nothing
	Worse than I already begin to imagine—
ROSAURA:	Yes, I will tell you—I do not know why
	I feel for you such deep respect, such veneration.
	Indeed, love, But how can I confess it?
	This man's clothing of mine is a disguise,
	I am not what I seem—now can you guess?

28

Astolfo has come here to marry Estrella—
Judge for yourself how he has wronged me!
Now you know everything!

(*Exit, with* PIPE)

CLOTALDO: Don't go away! Wait—listen—!
What a bewildering maze! And not a clue for
    reason to hold on to!
It is *my* honour that has been tainted!
The enemy is powerful, I am a vassal, she a
    woman!
Heaven may provide a solution,
But it is hard to see how even Heaven can
With nothing in the world but prodigies,
The sky full of portents, and all in chaos.

ACT TWO

Scene One

BASILIO, CLOTALDO.

CLOTALDO: All has been done as you ordered, Sire.

BASILIO: I wish to hear in detail, Clotaldo.

CLOTALDO: I will tell you everything, Sire, from the
beginning.
I gave him the drugged drink, as you
instructed,
An infusion of herbs, whose irresistible and
secret power
Takes away a man's faculties of reason and
speech,
Robs him of his senses,
Turns him into a living corpse, without will
or consciousness.
How is this possible? Useless to enquire:
Medicine makes empirical use of many of
nature's secrets,
As experience so often reminds us.
Every animal, plant and mineral
Has qualities peculiar to itself;
And if human wickedness has recorded a
thousand deadly poisons,
There is nothing, surely, so very surprising
In the less violent effects of the narcotics.
Some drugs cause death, and others only sleep;
This is beyond question, abundantly proved
by practice

31

And in no way contrary to reason; there we
must leave it.

I went down, then, to Segismundo's prison
Taking with me an opiate of poppy and
henbane.
We talked for a while of poetry and science
(For he has studied in the divine school of the
silent mountains and skies,
And there learned his rhetoric from the birds
and beasts)
And presently, so as to prepare his mind for
the test you have devised,
I led our conversation to the theme of the
eagle's flight:
Now, scorning the element of air,
She soars into the highest, the fiery sphere, a
comet of feathered lightening.
I praised her proud aspiring,
'Rightly indeed' I said 'is the eagle honoured
as queen of the birds!'
That was enough for him;
On the theme of royalty he speaks with
arrogant ambition,
(For, of course, his royal blood stirs in
him,
Arousing in him the desire for greatness)
And he replied, 'To think,
'Even in the restless republic of the birds
'There are some who must obey! There is
comfort for me in that,
'For if I am a slave, I am so only by compul-
sion;
'For by my own free will I would not submit
'To any man yet born!'

When I saw that the theme of his grievance had
    worked upon him,
I offered him the drink; no sooner had he
    emptied the cup
Then all his strength relaxed, and he fell
    asleep.
He shuddered, as if a deadly cold had passed
    through his veins,
And if I had not known that this was only
    apparent death,
I would not have believed him still alive.

At this moment the servants whom you had
    sent for him arrived,
Lifted him into the carriage, and brought him
    to your apartments.
There everything had been prepared
To receive him with the dignity due to his
    rank.
There he is lying now, on your bed of state,
And when the strength of the narcotic is spent
He will awake, attended as if he were yourself.
Your instructions, Sire, have been carried our
    to the letter.

And now, if I may claim in return a small
    favour,
I should only like to ask you—forgive my
    liberty—
To tell me what your motives are—why
Have you brought Segismundo to the palace
    in this way?

BASILIO: Your question is understandable, Clotaldo.
All the astrological indications, as you know,
Threaten my son Segismundo with endless
    misfortune and tragedy.

I wish to discover whether the heavens, which
    never lie—
And they gave proof enough of their terrible
    supremacy
At Segismundo's birth—can be circumvented,
Through courage, through prudence; or can
    at least be mitigated,
Tempered somewhat. Man, after all, is master
    of his fate.
Therefore I wish to try an experiment:
I bring him here; he learns that he is my
    son;
He is given an opportunity to put his powers
    to the test.
If he passes this trial, acts with magnanimity,
He shall reign; but if he is cruel and tyrannous
He shall go back to his chains. But, you will
    ask,
Why was he carried here in sleep, unconscious?
I will answer that question too:
If today Segismundo were to learn that he is
    my son
And find himself back in prison and misery
    tomorrow,
What would become of him? He would be in
    despair,
No consolation would be left him; but, as
    things are,
I have left a door open for a remedy; because,
    if that should happen,
We can tell him that all he saw was only a
    dream.
Thus my plan fulfils a double purpose:
On the one hand it enables us to examine his
    nature;

34

For when he wakes he will act according to
his will and disposition.
On the other, it allows a possibility, if he fails,
And finds himself, after being obeyed as a
prince,
Back in his prison,—of comfort;
For he will believe that it was all a dream.
And he would be right, Clotaldo, he would
be right:
For in this world every man who lives is only
dreaming!

CLOTALDO: I could think of many arguments to prove you
mistaken.
However, there is no help for it now.
It seems the Prince has awakened
And is coming this way—

BASILIO: Then I will retire.
Go to him, as his tutor, and tell him the truth:
No doubt he is bewildered and confused.

CLOTALDO: Have I then your permission to tell him
everything?

BASILIO: Yes, tell him all! For if he is forewarned
The danger may be more easily averted.

(*Exit* BASILIO)

Scene Two

Enter PIPER.

PIPER: (*aside*) A young lady-errant
Who is much too new-fangled
With her man's weapons
Will beat me for this;
But it's worth a few blows
To see what will happen.

I'm a poor lad, but wide—
So I see all the shows
Without buying a seat.
Do you know how I do it?
By cheek—that's my ticket!

CLOTALDO: Here comes Piper, the servant
Of that trader in misfortunes
Who has carried my dishonour
Across the Polish frontier.
Well, Piper, what's your news?

PIPER: My news Sir, is,
That the lady Rosaura,
Reassured by your kindness
And promise of vengeance
Has put on her real clothes.

CLOTALDO: She has done well;
She should not appear frivolous.

PIPER: And—this is the latest—
My lady is saying
That she is your niece—
—Her clever idea—
Has assumed a new name,
And lives at the Palace
As lady-in-waiting
To Princess Estrella.

LOTALDO:	I am glad of that too; It is right that on my account She should be honoured.
IPER:	One more piece of news Sir! She hopes that you'll find A good opportunity Soon, to avenge Your niece's good name!
CLOTALDO:	Again she is right. Time must bring the occasion.
IPER:	And my last piece of news— My lady—your niece— Is waited on hand and foot Like a princess! But I, her companion Am dying of hunger! Nobody cares What happens to me! They forget that if I Where to tell what I know To the King, to Astolfo, To Infanta Estrella, I could pipe up A good many secrets! Servants and pipers Don't take kindly to silence, And were I to sing, *Dawn's clarion shall not louder crow* *Than Piper's song shall ring.*
CLOTALDO:	You are perfectly right; I'll attend to your grievance, Meanwhile, I engage you!
PIPER:	Just in the nick of time! And here comes Segismundo.

Scene Three

Enter MUSICIANS, SEGISMUNDO, COURTIERS.

SEGISMUNDO: Great Heaven! What am I seeing?
What is all this?
I would be more willing to admire
If I were able to believe my eyes!
I, in the splendour of a palace? Dressed in
brocade and satin?
I, attended by courtiers, so handsome, so
deferential?
I, waking in such a bed as this?
I, with all these people helping me to dress?
Suppose I say that this is all a dream?
No—no. That would be mere self-deception,
For I am awake and know it!
I am Segismundo, am I not?
Heaven enlighten me!
Some change must have come over me while
I slept!
Some inexplicable trick of fantasy
Which is the reason why I find myself here!

Well, be that as it may,
Why, after all, should I let it trouble me?
Let them wait upon me, and come what may!

1st COURTIER: (*Aside to* 2nd COURTIER *and* PIPER)
He seems quite melancholy!

2nd COURTIER: Who would not be, in his position?

PIPER: Not me, for one!

2nd COURTIER: You speak to him.

1st COURTIER: Sire—shall they play again?

SEGISMUNDO: No, I don't want any more singing.

2nd COURTIER: You seem sad, and we are anxious to please
you.

38

SEGISMUNDO: Their voices do not please my sorrow.
I enjoy the sound only of martial music!
CLOTALDO: Sire! I kiss your hand!
Let me be the first to offer you my homage!
SEGISMUNDO: Clotaldo! Is it possible?
How comes it that my gaoler greets me with
deference?
What has happened?
CLOTALDO: You may well be amazed, and asking yourself
many questions
Concerning the great changes that your new
estate has brought;
But now, allow me to dispel your doubts.
I must inform Your Highness, you are Prince
and Heir Apparent
Of Poland. But—this also I must tell you—
You are by fate predestined
From the day the royal bays shall crown your
kingly forehead,
To bring disaster and tragedy upon the
Empire!
Yet — since every man is master of his
fate—
In hope that your free-will may triumph over
your stars,
You have been carried, in sleep, from the
Tower to the Royal Palace;
And presently the King, your royal father,
and my master,
Will visit you, and tell you more.
SEGISMUNDO: You infamous, vile traitor!
Now that I know who I am, I need no further
proof—
This very instant you shall feel my royal
anger!

39

	You have been a traitor to your country
	To conceal me, to deny me, against justice
	and reason, my rights!
CLOTALDO:	I a traitor!
SEGISMUNDO:	Did you not flout the law?
	Because you are a King's flatterer, you were
	cruel!
	Now kingship, the law, and I myself decree
	That you shall die at my hands!
2nd COURTIER:	Your Highness!
SEGISMUNDO:	Let none interfere! It will be useless!
	By God, I warn you, if you dare to come
	between us,
	I will throw you out of the window!
2nd COURTIER:	Flee, Clotaldo!
CLOTALDO:	Beware, Segismundo! Your overweening
	pride
	Proves that you are dreaming, and do not
	know it!
2nd COURTIER:	Remember, Sire—
SEGISMUNDO:	Away!
2nd COURTIER:	—that he only obeyed the King!
SEGISMUNDO:	In what is unjust, kings should not be obeyed!
	And was I not, besides, his Prince?
2nd COURTIER:	It was not for Clotaldo to question his
	instructions.
SEGISMUNDO:	You contradict me? Are you out of love with
	your life?
PIPER:	(*to* 2nd COURTIER) You are in the wrong,
	And everything the Prince says is quite
	true!
2nd COURTIER:	Who gave you permission to open your
	mouth?
PIPER:	I took it!
SEGISMUNDO:	Who are you? You may speak!

PIPER: A butter-in, Your Highness, that's what I am!
             I'm the world's widest boy!
SEGISMUNDO: In my new world, you are the only one I like!
PIPER: All Segismundos like me, Your Highness!

Scene Four

Enter ASTOLFO

ASTOLFO: Prince, this day is blessed indeed,
For your advent like the sun
Ascending from the mountain's bosom
Sheds its beams on our horizon.
Rise, sun of Poland! Though so late
The shining laurel crowns your brow,
May it later far be faded!

SEGISMUNDO: God keep you!

ASTOLFO: The fact that you are unaware
To whom you speak alone excuses
The incivility of your greeting.
I am Astolfo, your first cousin,
And Prince of Muscovy. We are peers!

SEGISMUNDO: What better can I wish you than God's keeping?
But since, along with all this boasting
Of who you are, you complain of my greeting,
Next time I meet you
I shall ask God *not* to keep you!

2nd COURTIER: (*to* ASTOLFO)
Your Highness must remember
He has been brought up in the wilds,
And therefore treats all men alike. (*to*
SEGISMUNDO) Your Highness,
The Prince Astolfo has privileges—

SEGISMUNDO: First he bores me with set speeches,
And then puts on his hat!

CLOTALDO: He is of high rank!

SEGISMUNDO: And I of higher!

2nd COURTIER: None the less, it would be fitting
There should be more civility
Between you two, than towards others!

SEGISMUNDO: Who told you to meddle with my affairs?

42

Enter ESTRELLA

ESTRELLA: Prince, I wish your Royal Highness
A thousand welcomes to the throne
That with thankfulness receives
The heir of Poland to his own.
Confounding those false auguries
May you reign in high renown
Not for years, but centuries!

SEGISMUNDO: (*to* PIPER) Tell me, who is this royal beauty?
This goddess before whose feet divine
The sky unrolls its glory? This lovely
    woman?

PIPER: The Infanta Estrella, Sire, your cousin.

SEGISMUNDO: Estrella! That means a star, but she is like the
    sun!
(*to* ESTRELLA) You may indeed congratulate
    me on this day's good fortune,
But for one reason alone—today I have seen
    you!
This meeting is itself a Prince's fortune!
Therefore I thank you, Princess, for your
    greeting.
Bright Estrella, morning star
Who with your rays kindle the sun's
    lantern,
Give me your snowy hand to kiss,
For from its immaculate chalice
The gentle morning breeze drinks freshness.

ESTRELLA: Sir, I beg you, be more formal!

ASTOLFO: If he takes her hand, I will lose my self-control!

2nd COURTIER: (*aside*) I can see what Astolfo is feeling—I'll
    say a word.

              (*to* SEGISMUNDO) Consider, Your Highness,
                it is not correct to be so free
              Especially when Astolfo—

SEGISMUNDO: Have I not told you already to mind your own
              business?

2nd COURTIER: I am only telling you, it is not done—

SEGISMUNDO: All this only serves to make me angry—
              What is done is what I choose to do!

2nd COURTIER: But, Your Highness, did I not hear you say
              That Kings should obey the laws of justice
              and reason?

SEGISMUNDO: You also heard me say that I would throw
              Any man who annoyed me out of the window!

2nd COURTIER: You can't do that to a man in my position!

SEGISMUNDO: No? By God, I'm going to try!

(*He seizes him and carries him out, followed by all the others, who reappear immediately*)

ASTOLFO: What a disgraceful scene!

ESTRELLA: Hurry! You must go and stop him!

SEGISMUNDO: He fell from the balcony into the water!
              Certainly it could be done!

ASTOLFO: That being so, Segismundo, I advise you to
              control your impulses,
              For the distance between man and animal is
              no less
              Than between mountain and palace.

SEGISMUNDO: Indeed? Then one day while you are indulging
              in solemn talk about perfection
              You may find you have no head to put your
              hat on!

Enter BASILIO

BASILIO: What has happened?

SEGISMUNDO: Happened? Nothing at all!

A man annoyed me, and I threw him out of the window!

PIPER: This is the King, you had better look out!

BASILIO: Has the first day of your arrival
Already cost a man his life?

SEGISMUNDO: He said it could not be done, and I won the wager.

BASILIO: A sorrowful day for me!
I came here to welcome you, as the Prince you are,
Hoping you would have heeded the warnings you received,
Hoping that I would see you mastering your stars, conquering fate,
And I find you instead acting like a savage:
Your first act has been a brutal murder:
How can I enfold you in my arms with love
Knowing that your arms have learned to kill?
Who can look without a shudder
At the bare dagger that has just inflicted a death-wound?
Now even the bravest can see without horror
The blood of a murdered man seeping into the ground.
And so it is with me: your arms have killed,
This room reeks of the blood you have shed.

45

In revulsion I draw back from your
    embrace!

My arms were open to clasp you

And enfold you lovingly—but I cannot touch
    you—

I will retire, in fear of your arms!

SEGISMUNDO: I have lived hitherto without that loving
    embrace,

And can continue to live as I have lived in the
    past.

A father who has been so heartless,

Who drove me from his side and reared me
    like a beast,

Treated me as a monster and desired my
    death,

Who all my life has denied me human
    rights,

What does it matter that he now withholds
    his embrace?

BASILIO: Would to Heaven that God had never allowed
    me

To give you life at all!

I would not then have lived to hear you utter
    such words,

Or to witness your insolence!

SEGISMUNDO: If you had never given me life, I should not
    blame you,

But since I live, I do, for having deprived me
    of life.

To give is the noblest, the most perfect act,

But the basest is to give in order to take
    away!

BASILIO: Is this your gratitude for a transformation

From a poor and obscure prisoner to a
    Prince?

SEGISMUNDO: Am I to thank you for that?
You, who have been the tyrant of my free will, are growing old, and weak:
In dying, what will you give that is not mine?
Since you are my father, and a king.
This greatness is my due by right of natural law,
And for this eminence, I am not indebted to you:
On the contrary—I might ask you to give me back
Those years you have robbed me of my liberty, life, and honour!
You should thank me for asking nothing of you, for you are the debtor!
BASILIO: Headstrong and savage! Heaven's prophecy is fulfilled!
I appeal to Heaven, you proud and haughty man!
For although you now know who you are,
Although you find yourself raised to the highest eminence,
I warn you—and you would do well to listen—
Be gentle; be humble; for it may be that you are dreaming,
Although you imagine yourself awake!
SEGISMUNDO: Dreaming, although I imagine myself awake?
No, I am not dreaming! I touch, and feel
What I am, and what I was! It is too late,
For you to repent it now! I know who I am,
And you can never, for all your prayers and sighs,
Rob me of my birth-right! I am heir to the crown,

47

And if in the past I accepted my imprisonment,
You must understand that I did not know
      what I was,
But now I know myself! I am nature's
      monster,
Part man, part beast!

Enter ROSAURA *in woman's clothes.*

ROSAURA: I must find the Infanta Estrella.
I hope I shall not meet Astolfo here,
For Clotaldo thinks it is better he should not
    see me;
I trust Clotaldo entirely, he is my protector,
To whom I owe my life, and honour.

PIPER: Tell me, your Highness,
Which of all the things you've been admiring
Do you like best?

SEGISMUNDO: Nothing surprises me;
It is all just as I imagined it would be.
One thing only I had not imagined—the
    beauty of woman.
Once I read in some book that man had
    received most care from the hands of God
For he is the earth's microcosm;
But now I wonder if it was not woman;
For woman is a tiny heaven; she enshrines
    beauty,
As far above man as heaven is above earth;
And most of all, she whom I now see!

ROSAURA: The Prince is here—I will withdraw.

SEGISMUNDO: Don't go, madam—wait—listen—
The sun must not rise and set in the same
    moment,
Dawn plunge into evening, noon to night—
You must not cut short the day! But who is
    this lady?

ROSAURA: (*aside*) I can neither believe my eyes, nor
    doubt them!

SEGISMUNDO: (*aside*) Once before I have seen this beauty!

49

ROSAURA: Once before I saw this proud magnificence
Humbled and degraded in a narrow prison
SEGISMUNDO: Now I have found my life! Woman—
I address you by the name most precious to
man—
Who are you? I have scarcely seen you
And yet it seems to me that I have worshipped
you for long;
And because I know that elsewhere I have
loved your beauty
I claim you mine!
What is your name? Who are you?
ROSAURA: (aside) He must not recognise me!
Only a humble lady in waiting to the Infanta
Estrella.
SEGISMUNDO: Don't say that! You must be the sun that
lights the star!
Her glory is a reflection from your beams.
Once in the kingdom of sweet scents, I saw
the rose
Enthroned as queen of all the orders of the
flowers,
For there, the fairest reigns;
And again, in the profound school of the
mines
I saw, among the stones, the most brilliant
Chosen as Emperor, the matchless diamond;
And in that high court
Where the ever-changing stars have their
republic,
I saw one chosen to be first, and king-like,
The morning star, the brightest.
Yes, and I have seen the sun
Summoning all the planets to his council,
But he, the day's great oracle

Presided over all.
And if among flowers, stars, jewels, planets
   and heavenly houses,
The most beautiful is preferred,
How can you serve a beauty less than your
   own?
You being rose, diamond, morning star, and
   sun?

Enter CLOTALDO, *in the wings.*

CLOTALDO: I should like to bring Segismundo to
reason;

For, after all, I brought him up. But what is
happening now?

ROSAURA: I am greatly honoured. I hope my silence is
eloquent.

When no reasonable answer can be made

He speaks best, Your Highness, who says
least.

SEGISMUNDO: You must not go—wait—

How can you leave me plunged in darkness?

ROSAURA: I ask leave, your Highness!

SEGISMUNDO: To leave me so abruptly

Is not to ask leave, but to take it!

ROSAURA: I must take it, if you will not give it.

SEGISMUNDO: Then you will force me from courtesy to
roughness;

For opposition works like poison on my
patience!

ROSAURA: Your patience may be poisoned by rage and
anger,

But these cannot touch my modesty and
honour!

SEGISMUNDO: Your words are melting away the awe I feel
for your beauty!

You challenge me to make you yield? Very
well—

I am much inclined to conquering the im-
possible!

I have thrown a man out of the window today
already

For saying it could not be done! And so, it
    would seem
If only to prove that I can, I must throw your
    honour
Out of the window!

CLOTALDO: This is too much! Heaven direct me!
Through mad passion a second time my
    honour is in danger!

ROSAURA: Ah! So the prophecy was true
That you would bring down ruin upon this
    kingdom
By crimes of treachery, violence and murder!
But what can be expected of such a monster—
Reckless, inhuman, cruel proud tyrant that
    you are,
Born among beasts, a man only in name!

SEGISMUNDO: It was in order to avoid such insults from you
That I was courteous, hoping by courtesy
To win your favour; but if in spite of that
You say that I am all these things, by God!
I will give you good reason for your insult!
You, there! Leave us alone here—shut that
    door!
Let no-one come in!

Exit PIPER *and* SERVANTS)

ROSAURA: (*aside*) I am lost! (*to* SEGISMUNDO) Please
    consider—

SEGISMUNDO: I am a tyrant! Too late to tame me now!

CLOTALDO: What a wild scene! I will prevent him
Even if he kills me! (*Enters*) Your Highness!
    Stop! Listen!

SEGISMUNDO: This is the second time you have angered me,
You miserable old fool! Are you not afraid of
    me?
What brought you here?

53

CLOTALDO:	The sound of your own voice!
	As you hope to reign, I beg you to be more gentle!
	You are cruel because you think you are the master,
	But what if this were to prove an illusion?
SEGISMUNDO:	You only enrage me when you preach disillusion!
	You will see when I kill you what is real!

(CLOTALDO *falls on his knees, and stops* SEGISMUNDO's *hand from drawing his sword*)

CLOTALDO:	Surely you will not kill a suppliant—
SEGISMUNDO:	Take your hand away!
CLOTALDO:	Not until others come to check your fury.
ROSAURA:	Help, for God's sake!
SEGISMUNDO:	Decrepit old fool, let go, I say!
	Or I will kill you with my hands, like this!
ROSAURA:	Come quickly! He is murdering Clotaldo!

(*Enter* ASTOLFO; *as* CLOTALDO *falls at his feet,* ASTOLFO *places himself between them.*)

ASTOLFO: But what is this, Your Royal Highness?
           Would you stain proud steel with an old man's
               frozen blood?
           Put up your sword!
SEGISMUNDO: No! Not before it is dyed with that infamous
               blood!
ASTOLFO: His life in now under my protection,
           My arrival is timely.
SEGISMUNDO: Timely indeed! Time for your death too!
           So I will avenge a past insult!
ASTOLFO: In defending my life, I do not offend the
               crown!
CLOTALDO: Spare his life, Astolfo!

Enter BASILIO, ESTRELLA *and* ATTENDANTS.

BASILIO: What is this? Drawn swords in our presence?

ESTRELLA: (*aside*) Astolfo! His presence reminds me of
my own grievance!

BASILIO: Well? What has occurred?

ASTOLFO: Nothing, Sire, since you have arrived.
(*All replace swords*)

SEGISMUNDO: A great deal Sire, your arrival notwith-
standing!
I wanted to kill that old grey-beard!

BASILIO: Have you no reverence for white hairs?

CLOTALDO: Sire, these white hairs are only mine—of no
consequence!

SEGISMUNDO: Why ask me to show reverence
For *his* white hairs, when even these (*to the*
KING)
May one day be brought low before my feet?
Remember, I have not yet taken my revenge
For the injustice of my up-bringing!

(*Exit* SEGISMUNDO)

BASILIO: Rather than wait for that event
You shall sleep again
And think that this has been
Like all the good things of the world,
Only a dream—

(*Exit* KING, CLOTALDO, SERVANTS)

ASTOLFO: How seldom does Fate lie
When it predicts misfortune,
For how unfailingly
Evils come to man,
Happiness, how rarely.
The best astrologer
Would only ills predict—
He would be always right.
The truth of this is clear
If you will but consider
Myself and Segismundo.
For him the horoscope
Foretold only disaster
And all foretold proved true.
My case is worse than his—
Fate wronged me with good omens,
For your eyes dart disdain,
They make the sun a shadow,
The fixed stars, transient!
Thus, Fate foretold for me
Wealth, applause and conquest,
Only to mislead me
With favours turned to scorn!

ESTRELLA: I do not doubt the truth
Of all your gallantries;
But they must be addressed
To that other lady
Whose portrait you were wearing
When, the other day;
You came to visit me.
These speeches are for her.
Go to her, Astolfo,
And ask her to reward you!

Gallantries and oaths
That have been paid to others
Are empty and invalid!

(ROSAURA, *off-stage*.)

ROSAURA: Now I know the worst!
            Thank God! My grief at last
            Must have an end, for this
            Is all that I could fear.

ASTOLFO: That picture shall give place—
            For I wear upon my heart
            The image of your beauty.
            The bright star banishes
            The shadow, as the sun
            Chases away the stars.
            I will bring the portrait.
            (*aside*) Forgive this crime, Rosaura,
            For it is one; but how seldom
            Are men or women true
            To absent loves, or more
            Faithful than I am now!

(*Approaching* ESTRELLA, *aside*)

ROSAURA: I heard nothing—
            I was only afraid that he would see me!

ESTRELLA: Astrea!

ROSAURA: Your Highness?

ESTRELLA: I am glad that you have come.
            In the short time I have known you
            I have grown fond of you;
            So, since you are what you are,
            I will venture to entrust you
            With a secret I have hidden
            Even from myself.

ROSAURA: I am at your service.

ESTRELLA: It is this; I will be brief.
            My cousin, Astolfo,

(I might simply say, my cousin,
For some things go without saying)
Is to marry me, if Heaven
Allows us to consign
These late troubles to oblivion.
But I must confess, it hurt me
That when first he called on me
He was wearing round his neck
The portrait of a lady.
Just now I spoke of it;
And, being in love with me,
And courteous and considerate,
He has gone to fetch it.

But I should be embarrassed
To take the portrait; please
Wait here till he returns,
Ask him to give it you.
I need say no more—
For you are beautiful,
And must know what love is—

Exit ESTRELLA

ROSAURA: Too well, Heaven knows!
Who, in my situation,
Could behave wisely or well,
Faced with such an ordeal!
Is any human being
In the whole wide world
More battered by the blows
Of unkind fate than I?
What am I to do?
What comfort can I find,
Among so many sorrows!
From my first misfortune
Every consequence,

Every happening or action
Has been unfortunate
For each follows from the last,
Heirs in direct succession.
Sorrows are like the Phoenix,
And each new sorrow's ashes
Keeps warm the funeral pyre.
Once a philosopher
Called misfortunes cowards—
They never come alone,
He said, but I would say,
Rather, that they are fearless,
Because they march straight on
And never call retreat.
Sorrows are companions
Who never will desert
Those who travel with them;
Untiring they'll pursue me
Until, mortally wounded
In death's arms they desert me.

What must I do today
In this new situation?
If I say who I am
Clotaldo will be angry,
And he has promised me
Honour and satisfaction
If I maintain my silence.
I owe him everything—
But when I see Astolfo
How then can I dissemble?
My voice, my speech, my eyes,
These I might disguise,
But how disguise my heart?
What shall I do? But why

Ask, since it is plain,
However much I may
Anticipate the moment,
Ponder, and think ahead,
When the occasion comes
Pride and pain alone
Will dictate my conduct.
Who can control sorrow?
No one! So I shall not
Rehearse what I will say.
Only let me end
Doubt and deceit together,
Once and for all; till then,
Heaven help me! Help me, Heaven!

Enter ASTOLFO, *bringing the portrait.*

ASTOLFO: Here, Madam, is the portrait—
              But . . . . . Good God!

ROSAURA: Why is your Highness surprised?
              Why astonished?

ASTOLFO: At seeing and hearing you, Rosaura.

ROSAURA: Rosaura? I, Rosaura?
              Your Highness is mistaken!
              You take me for another lady.
              I am Astrea, and in my obscure position
              Cannot deserve the honour of embarrassing
                  you!

ASTOLFO: Stop pretending, Rosaura! The heart never
                  lies.
              I see you as Astrea, but love you as Rosaura!

ROSAURA: I do not understand Your Highness,
              And that being so, do not know what to
              answer.
              All I have to say is that Estrella
              That bright star, who must be Venus herself
              Asked me to wait for you here, on her behalf,
              To receive from you a portrait—
              A reasonable request—
              And to take it to her.
              Those are Estrella's wishes, Sir;
              For the trifles that I suffer
              Are by the agency of that sovereign star.

ASTOLFO: How hard you are trying to pretend, my dear
                  Rosaura,
              But not succeeding.
              Your eyes are out of tune with your voice—
              But there must be discordant notes

	When the instrument plays a tune
	False to all the heart is feeling.
ROSAURA:	I am only waiting for the portrait,
	As I have already said.
ASTOLFO:	Very well,
	Since you wish to keep up the pretence
	To the last, I will act too.
	Astrea, please inform the Princess
	That I honour her too greatly
	To send her a mere copy,
	So I send her something better,
	The inestimable and rare original—
	You yourself can take it with you,
	For you carry it everywhere.
ROSAURA:	When a man of pride
	Sets out to accomplish
	Some particular quest,
	If he fails to keep his word
	He will feel it a dishonour
	Even if he returns
	Having negotiated
	For a more precious prize.
	I have come for the portrait,
	And though I may go back
	With the original
	—Which indeed is far more precious—
	I should go back slighted.
	And so, Your Highness,
	Give me that portrait!
	For I will not leave without it.
ASTOLFO:	But how can you take it
	If I refuse to give it?
ROSAURA:	Like this! Let it go, you wretch!
(Tries to snatch it)	
ASTOLFO:	You see, struggling is useless!

ROSAURA:	My God, it shall never be In another woman's hands!
ASTOLFO:	How fierce you are!
ROSAURA:	And you, how perfidious!
ASTOLFO:	That's enough, my dear Rosaura!
ROSAURA:	I yours? You base liar!

Enter ESTRELLA.

ESTRELLA: Astrea, Astolfo—what is going on?

ASTOLFO: (*aside to* ROSAURA) Here is Estrella coming.

ROSAURA: Love give me inspiration!
I must get back my portrait!
Madam, let me explain!

ASTOLFO: Be careful what you say.

ROSAURA: You told me to wait here for Astolfo
And ask him for a portrait
That he had gone to bring you.
You know, when one's alone
One thought leads to another—
I happened to remember
That I was carrying
A portrait of myself.
I took it from my sleeve,
And I was looking at it
When Astolfo came,
It slipped out of my hand,
He picked it up, and now
He won't return it to me,
And won't give his up either,
For all that I can say,
And so I grew impatient
Just now, and tried to snatch it—

That's mine, now, in his hand—
Look at it for yourself—
You see, it is my likeness.

ESTRELLA: Astolfo, give it to me.

ASTOLFO: Madam—

ESTRELLA: It certainly
Does justice to your beauty!

ROSAURA:	It is like me, is it not?
ESTRELLA:	Who could doubt it?
ROSAURA:	Now ask him for the other!
ESTRELLA:	Take your portrait, and leave us.
ROSAURA:	Now come what may
	I have retrieved my portrait.

(*Exit*)

ESTRELLA: Now, please, give me the portrait
For which I asked, because
Although I don't intend
To speak to you or see you
Ever again, I do
Intend to have that portrait,
If for no better reason
Than that I was so foolish
As to ask you for it.

ASTOLFO: I can see no way out (*aside*)
(*to* ESTRELLA)
Beautiful Estrella,
Much as I wish to serve
Your will in every way,
Yet you must forgive me
If in this case, I
Am not, after all,
Able to oblige you,
Because—

ESTRELLA: You are a base
And vulgar lover! I
No longer want it now,
Nor wish to be reminded
I ever asked you for it.

Exit ESTRELLA

ASTOLFO: Don't go—wait a moment!
Please listen—Oh, Rosaura,
Whence and how and why
Did you appear today
At the court of Poland
To bring us both to ruin!
(*Exit*)

The PRINCE's *prison, in the Tower.*
SEGISMUNDO, *as at the beginning of the play, dressed in skins,
shackled, lying on the floor.* CLOTALDO *and two* SERVANTS:
PIPER.

CLOTALDO:	Here you must leave him, All his pride ending Where it began.
1ST SERVANT:	His fetters are just as they were.
PIPER:	Sleep on, Segismundo! Troubles can't hurt A sleeping man. So your splendours all Are faded and gone! Life is a shadow, And death holds the candle.
CLOTALDO:	Such a philosopher should have a quiet cell Where he can discourse at leisure. (*to* SERVANTS) This is the man you are to imprison: Put him in that dungeon.
PIPER:	Why me?
CLOTALDO:	A Piper who knows secrets Must be kept where no secrets can blow away.
PIPER:	I ask you, did I try To kill my father? No! Did I Throw that amateur Icarus Out of the window? No! Was I Ever given to having dreams? Then why do they put me in prison?
CLOTALDO:	Because Pipers pipe!

69

PIPER: I promise,
I'll be a bag-piper from now on—
A horrid noise the bag-pipes make,
So I promise I'll keep mum!
(*Exit*)

BASILIO *enters, muffled in his cloak.*

BASILIO:	Clotaldo!
CLOTALDO:	Sire!
	Your majesty here in disguise!
BASILIO:	My foolish curiosity has brought me
	To see how poor Segismundo will act when he awakens.
CLOTALDO:	There he lies,
	Reduced to his old condition once again.
BASILIO:	Poor, unfortunate prince,
	Born in an evil hour! Go, now, and wake him:
	The opium has taken away his strength.
CLOTALDO:	He is restless, Sire; talks in his sleep.
BASILIO:	What can he be dreaming? Let us listen!
SEGISMUNDO:	*(asleep)* A merciful prince is he who punishes tyrants!
	Let Clotaldo die at my hands and my father kiss my feet!
CLOTALDO:	He threatens me with death!
BASILIO:	And me with dishonour!
CLOTALDO:	He intends to take my life!
BASILIO:	And plots my overthrow!
SEGISMUNDO:	Let my unrivalled valour
	Step on to the great stage
	Of the world's vast theatre,
	That vengeance may be mine!
	They shall see Prince Segismundo's triumph over his father!
	(He wakes)
	But—what has happened? Where am I
BASILIO:	He must on no account see me—

Clotaldo, you know what to do; I shall listen
from here.
(*conceals himself*)

SEGISMUNDO: Can this be myself?
Is it I who am imprisoned, and in fetters?

Surely this is my tower, my sepulchre!
God knows what things I have been
dreaming!

CLOTALDO: Now I must play the disenchanter.
It is time to wake! (*to* SEGISMUNDO)

SEGISMUNDO: It is indeed time to wake!

CLOTALDO: Are you going to sleep all day?
I left you watching an eagle that flew by,
Soaring idly. Have you not woken
Since I left you?

SEGISMUNDO: No. Even now
I am not awake! To the best of my under-
standing
I am still asleep. For if what seemed palpable
and certain
Proves to be a dream,
What I now see is no less unsure—
No wonder if I am overcome,
Since when I sleep I see that I dream when I
am waking.

CLOTALDO: Will you not tell me your dream?

SEGISMUNDO: If we are to suppose, then,
That it was a dream, I will tell you
Not what I dreamed, but what in that dream
I experienced.
I awoke, and found myself (what a cruel
deception!)
On a bed, whose flowered coverlets
Spring herself might have woven.

72

Scores of courtiers were kneeling
At my feet, called me their Prince,
Brought me fine clothes, and jewels.
And then, Clotaldo, you came
And turned my confusion to joy
By telling me my good fortune—
That I, whom now you see,
Was Prince of Poland!

CLOTALDO: You must have rewarded me highly for that!

SEGISMUNDO: On the contrary;
Because you had been a hardened and shameless traitor
I tried, on two occasions, to murder you!

CLOTALDO: Were you so cruel to me?

SEGISMUNDO: I was the master there, and took revenge on all.
Only one I loved—a woman. That love must have been real
For everything else has faded, only that love remains.

CLOTALDO: (*aside*) The King, saddened by what he has heard, has slipped away.
(*to* PRINCE) We were talking of that eagle, and so you dreamed of empire
But even in a dream, Segismundo, would it not have been better
To show gratitude to your old schoolmaster,
Who brought you up, and loved you? For even in dreams, you know,
Good deeds are never lost.
(*Exit*)

SEGISMUNDO: Yes, that is true;
Then let me transcend this bestial condition.

73

Anger, selfish ambition, lest I should dream
    again.
And so perhaps I shall; for we live in a world
    so strange
That to live is only to dream.
He who lives, dreams his life
Until he wakes. This
Experience has taught me.
The king dreams he is king,
And, under that delusion,
He orders, rules, disposes,
Until all the applause
That is only lent to him
Is scattered on the winds,
And death turns him to ashes.
What an unkind fate!
Who would wish to be king,
Knowing that he must wake
From his dream in the sleep of death?
The rich man dreams of wealth to his heart's
    content,
The poor man dreams he suffers hardship and
    poverty,
The prosperous dreams his prosperity,
The labourer his toils and hopes;
Injured and injurer dream of wrongs,
And everyone in the world
Dreams that he is what he is!
This, no-one understands!
I dream that I am here,
Loaded with chains, or dream
That I see myself in some other,
More illustrious, part.
What is life? a delirium!
What is life? illusion,

A shadow, a fiction,
Whose greatest good is nothing,
Because life is a dream!
Even dreams are only dreams.

ACT THREE

Scene One

PIPER (*alone*)

PIPER: This must be an enchanted tower,
I shouldn't wonder.
They're killing me for what I know!
For a man with an appetite like mine
It's grim death to be alive!
So what will they do to me, I ask you,
For what I don't know? That's a question!
Am I sorry for myself?
You may as well say 'yes' at once,
For you'll have to believe me in the end—
I'll pipe up, or my name's not Piper!
Now if I were to tell you
Who I keep company with here—
I can't bring myself to say it—
Mice and spiders! They're the birds!
And last night's dreams have filled my head
With trumpets and hallucinations,
Crosses, processions, flagellations!
Some raise their whips, some bring them down!
Some faint to see how the others bleed!
And I'm faint too—faint with starvation!
For here in prison, on the lunch menu,
Everything's 'off'; the same for supper.
Silence is blessed, so they say;
If so, my saint is Blessed Silence:

I keep his fast, but when's his feast-day?
All the same, it serves me right:
Servants who keep their mouths shut tight
Deserve everything they get.

Scene Two

Enter SOLDIERS.

1st SOLDIER:	(*within*) He's in this tower!
	This way, all of you, break down the door!
PIPER:	It must be me they're after!
	They said 'He's here!'
	What can they want me for?
1st SOLDIER:	This way—in here.
2nd SOLDIER:	This is he!
PIPER:	No he's not!
SOLDIERS:	Sire!
PIPER:	Drunk, obviously!
1st SOLDIER:	You are our rightful Prince!
	We will not recognize
	Admit or tolerate
	Any other leader.
	We want no foreigner!
	Allow us to salute you!
SOLDIERS:	Long live our noble Prince!
PIPER:	Good God! So they mean business!
	It seems to be the custom in this foreign country
	To arrest a different person every day,
	First make him a Prince, then put him in this tower!
	You see it happening all the time! That's what it is,
	And now it's my turn!
SOLDIERS:	Give us your hands!
PIPER:	Oh no you don't, I need them
	Myself, and it's not right
	To mutilate my royal person!

79

2nd SOLDIER:	We informed the King your father
	Openly to his face
	That we would recognize
	Only the rightful Prince
	As the Heir Apparent.
2nd SOLDIER:	We don't want that Russian!
PIPER:	You said that to my father?
	Have you no respect?
	You're cads, that's what you are!
2nd SOLDIER:	Our loyalty compelled us.
PIPER:	In that case I forgive you.
2nd SOLDIER:	Come and save your Empire!
	Long live Segismundo!
ALL:	Hurrah for Segismundo!
PIPER:	(*aside*) They called me Segismundo!
	That must be the name
	Of all these puppet princes!

Scene Three

Enter SEGISMUNDO

SEGISMUNDO: Who called for Segismundo?
PIPER: So I'm dropped already!
1st SOLDIER: Who is Segismundo?
SEGISMUNDO: I am.
2nd SOLDIER: (*to* PIPER) You fool.
How dare you play the imposter
And pose as Segismundo!
PIPER: I never! It was you
Who Segismundo'd me!
Who's daring and who's fooling?
Not me! Fool yourself!
1st SOLDIER: Noble Prince Segismundo,
For you must be our Prince,
From all that we have heard
Of Your Highness' person—
(Which indeed inspires our faith
And compels us to acclaim you)
Your father, King Basilio,
Fearing lest Heaven fulfil
The fate it pre-ordained
And he himself be conquered
And lie vanquished at your feet,
Now intends to rob you
Of your freedom and your rights,
Give your kingdom to Astolfo
Duke of Muscovy.
He has summoned Parliament,
And all the people know
What he intends to do.
They demand their natural king,
And not a foreigner!

81

So we have come to free you
And bring you from your prison.
We don't care for the stars!
The army is behind you,
To take you from this Tower
And retrieve from a tyrant
The Imperial Crown and Sceptre.
Out on the mountainside
A mighty army stands,
Outlaws, and partisans.
They are waiting now, and cheering,
Listen to their shouting!
Liberty awaits you.

VOICES: *(off)* Hurrah! Segismundo!
SEGISMUNDO: What is this? Heaven,
Do you want me again
To dream a dream
Of greatness, that time
Will once more shatter?
Do you want me to see
How the phantoms and shadows
Of pomp and majesty
In the wind scatter?
Do you want me again
To know disillusion,
Encounter the hazards
To which men are born,
Eager to meet them,
But too weak to master?
No—I refuse,
I will not again
Be bound by my fate
For now I have learned
That this life is a dream.
Away, you shadows,

82

Who today assume
Voices and bodies
To deceive mortal sense
Though in truth you possess
Neither bodies nor voices!
I do not want
A play of kingship,
A fantasm of pomp,
Illusions that fade
At the lightest breath
Like the almond-tree
That blossoms too early,
Too rashly forces
Those rosy buds
That unfold their light
And delicate beauty
To wilt without warning
At the first wind
And always to scatter
Their petals too soon.
I know you, Heaven,
And how it befalls
With those who sleep!
For me, in vain
Is all your seeming,
For already I know,
Too bitterly know it,
That life is a dream!

2nd SOLDIER: If you think we are fooling you,
Look over there,
Towards the mountain—
There are the soldiers
Awaiting your orders.

SEGISMUNDO: Once before
I saw such things,

Distinctly and clearly
As now I see them,
But all was a dream!

2nd SOLDIER: My Lord, great events
Cast their shadow before—
Your dream was prophetic.

SEGISMUNDO: Yes, you are right.
Perhaps a foreshadowing,
And, perhaps, true.
Then since life is so short,
My soul, let us dream,
Let us dream life again,
But always remember
That we must awake
In the moment of pleasure.
This, never forget,
And the fading, foreknown,
Can bring no disillusion;
For we may mock
At an evil foreseen.
What though the powers
That we enjoy
Are only on loan
And must be returned
To those who lend them?
Let us dare all!

Subjects, I thank you
All for your loyalty.
You will find, in me,
A leader, who,
Strong and fearless,
Will free you today
From the foreigner's yoke!
Summon to arms!

Soon you will witness
My valour undaunted.
I will take up my sword
Against my father,
And prove how true
Were the stars, in their oracles;
For I will see him
Kneel at my feet!
(*aside*)
Better, perhaps
To have held my peace;
For what if I waken
Before this is done?

ALL: Hurrah! Segismundo! (etc)

Scene Four

Enter CLOTALDO

CLOTALDO: What is the meaning of this noise and shouting?

SEGISMUNDO: Clotaldo . . .

CLOTALDO: My Lord.
(*aside*) I will be the first
On whom he will wreck his vengeance.

PIPER: I bet he will throw him down these rocks.
(*exit*)

CLOTALDO: I kneel at your royal feet—
I know, only to die.

SEGISMUNDO: Father, rise,
Rise from the ground;
For you must be the compass,
The leader and guide
To whom I entrust
All my hopes of success.
My upbringing
I owe to your loyalty—
Come to my arms!

CLOTALDO: What do you mean?

SEGISMUNDO: That I am dreaming
And mean to do good—
For even in dreams
Good deeds are not lost!

CLOTALDO: Then, my Lord, if your resolution
Is now to do right, it will not offend you
If I ask your leave to do right on my side too.
You are warring today against your father:
    I cannot serve you
Against my king, nor advise you.
So again I kneel: now kill me.

SEGISMUNDO: Ungrateful traitor!
(aside) But I must control my anger
For I do not know yet whether I am awake!
(to CLOTALDO*)*
Clotaldo—I envy and admire your courage,
And thank you for it; go now and serve the
    King.
We will meet on the field.
(to SOLDIERS*)* You—call to arms!

CLOTALDO: I kiss your feet!
(Exit)

SEGISMUNDO: So, Fortune, we go to reign!
If I am asleep, don't wake me!
And if awake, don't let me sleep again!
But, waking or sleeping, one thing only
Matters: to act rightly;
If awake, because acts are real,
If dreaming, to win friends for the time of
    awaking.

Room in the Royal Palace.

BASILIO *and* ASTOLFO.

BASILIO: Who, Astolfo, by diplomacy and prudence
Can stop the fury of a bolting horse?
Who can check the flow of a flooded torrent
Plunging headlong through its gorges to the
    ocean?
What hero will stand in the path of an
    avalanche
To stop the rock broken loose from a
    mountain summit?
To turn the fury of an excited crowd
Is something still more difficult. Listen
To the two-voiced rumour of the mob!
From the mountains you can hear the
    echoes—
Some cry 'Astolfo', others 'Segismundo'.
My throne, too, has become ambiguous,
Divided, as the people are, by conflict,
The stage of a tragedy played out by inexor-
    able fate.

ASTOLFO: Sire, today let us postpone the celebrations,
All the rejoicings with which so generously
You promised to honour me; because, if
    Poland
(Which I hope to rule) refuses to obey me
It is only in order that I may first deserve her.
Give me a horse, and then let the proud
    thunderer
Come down from the mountains like a
    lightning-flash!

        Exit

BASILIO: How, against the infallible, can we defend
ourselves?
And what is foretold is full of gravest menace,
If fate is inexorable, there can be no defence
And the man who tries the hardest to avert it
Only the more surely foresees his own
destruction.
The laws of destiny are cruel! Terrible to
witness
How, fleeing from danger we run into danger,
And I, by seeking to save myself, am lost—
I, I myself have destroyed my kingdom!

Scene Six

Enter ESTRELLA.

ESTRELLA: Sire, unless with your presence you can quell
              The riots spreading in the streets and squares
              You will see your kingdom afloat on scarlet
                  waves
              Dyed with the purple of its own blood.
              How lamentably all is turned to tragedy and
                  disaster!
              Your empire is in its death-throes—violent,
              All sights are terrible, all sounds apall.
              The sun is outraged and the wind infected,
              Every stone marks a grave-plot, every flower
              Grows for some funeral wreath; and not a
                  house
              But now has become a vault and sepulchre;
              And all your soldiers are corpses walking to
                  the battlefield!

Enter CLOTALDO

CLOTALDO:	Thank God I have reached you alive!
BASILIO:	Now, Clotaldo, what news of Segismundo?
CLOTALDO:	The mob, that blind unbridled monster,
	Has forced the Tower, and from its fastness
	Loosed the Prince; now for a second time
	He who knows who he is, and now gives proof
	Of his true nature, declaring boldly
	That he will fulfil the word that Heaven has
	spoken!
BASILIO:	Bring me a horse, for I myself
	Will take the field,
	And my ungrateful son shall yield!
	In defence of throne and crown
	Let steel prevail where wisdom failed!
ESTRELLA:	Then I will like Bellona ride
	By royal Helios' side.
	There, my name's pride
	Aspires, with pinions spread,
	To soar, like Pallas, by the sun's chariot.

(ROSAURA, *stopping* CLOTALDO)

ROSAURA:	I know you are impatient
	To go and join the fighting,
	But listen to me, I beg you!
	You know how I reached Poland,
	Poor, unknown, unhappy,
	You gave me your protection,
	The shelter of your honour—
	You told me I must live
	In the Palace in disguise,
	Conceal my jealousy,
	Avoid meeting Astolfo;

Unluckily he saw me—
But he tramples on my honour!
He goes to meet Estrella
Every evening in the garden;
This, after seeing me!
But now I have the key
Of the garden, I can give you
The opportunity
At last, to right my wrongs,
Your pride, courage and strength
May restore me my good name
Now, for you gave your word
To avenge me by his death!

CLOTALDO: It is true, Rosaura, that since first I saw you
I have tried in every way to help you,
(To this your tears bear witness:)
First, I made you change your clothes
So that Astolfo should not, seeing you
Dressed as a man, think you immodest,
Casting your reputation to the winds.
I have been pondering, meanwhile,
How best to help you to redeem
Your good name; even considering
—So much your honour means to me—
Killing Astolfo! Wicked folly!
True, since he is not my king,
I owe no allegiance to his person,
Nor do I fear him—and indeed
I had made up my mind to kill him
When Segismundo threatened me.
Then, risking his own life, Astolfo
Came, in pure friendship, to my aid.
Now, how can I, in gratitude
Repay the man who saved my life
With death? Thus I am torn in two

Between my affection for you, my debt to
    him:
One or the other I must repay—
I saved your life, but he saved mine.
To you I am bound, since I have helped you,
Bound to him, since he helped me;
In which predicament, it is clear
That any course must bring dishonour.

ROSAURA: For a man of your rank
To give must be noble,
But base to receive.
By this argument, therefore,
You should not be grateful
To him, for by giving
He made you indebted
To him for your life,
Which is base, whereas I
Made you noble by giving.
He has done you an injury,
Then; but to me
You yourself are indebted,
For you gave to me
What he gave to you,
So from this it is plain
You must defend me,
For my claim is the stronger,
Since he is the giver
And I the receiver.

CLOTALDO: Magnanimity is the virtue of the giver,
But gratitude of the receiver.
To give is my custom; I am accounted
    generous.
But I aspire to deserve no less
To be called grateful: for only so
Is to receive as honourable as to give.

ROSAURA: When I received life from you
You yourself told me
To live without honour
Was not to live truly.
Then you have given me
Nothing—the life
That you gave me was nothing!
You said so yourself;
And if you say truly
That giving is nobler
Than gratitude, surely
You should practise the greater
Virtue, be liberal
First, and only
Afterwards grateful.

CLOTALDO: Very well; won by your argument I consent
First, Rosaura, to be liberal:
I will endow you with my whole fortune,
And you shall retire to a convent; this solution
Is well thought of; for thus you avoid the
guilt of a crime
And at the same time find shelter in a
sanctuary.
It is not for me, by birth a noble
To augment the tragedy of civil war.
Thus, by the solution I have decided upon,
I remain loyal to the King, liberal towards
you, grateful to Astolfo.
Your are free to decide;
But see that this remains a secret between us.
God knows I could not do more were I your
father!

ROSAURA: Were you my father
Perhaps I should tolerate
This bitter insult;

	But since you are not
	I will not endure it!
CLOTALDO:	Then what do you propose?
ROSAURA:	To kill the Duke!
CLOTALDO:	Can a woman who never
	Knew her own father
	Be so courageous?
ROSAURA:	Certainly!
CLOTALDO:	Who
	Sponsors your action?
ROSAURA:	My own good name!
CLOTALDO:	But consider, Astolfo
	Will soon be—
ROSAURA:	My honour
	Takes precedence!
CLOTALDO:	Your King,
	And Estrella's husband!
ROSAURA:	By God, he shall not!
CLOTALDO:	You are mad!
ROSAURA:	I know it!
CLOTALDO:	Control it!
ROSAURA:	I cannot!
CLOTALDO:	Then you will lose—
ROSAURA:	I know—
CLOTALDO:	—life and honour.
ROSAURA:	I know—
CLOTALDO:	Then your aim is—
ROSAURA:	My death!
CLOTALDO:	That is spite!
ROSAURA:	It is honour!
CLOTALDO:	Folly!
ROSAURA:	Courage!
CLOTALDO:	Hysteria!
ROSAURA:	No, it is rage,
	It is fury!

95

CLOTALDO:	Can nothing Curb this blind passion?
ROSAURA:	Nothing!
CLOTALDO:	Who will help you?
ROSAURA:	Only myself!
CLOTALDO:	Is there no way to stop you?
ROSAURA:	None!
CLOTALDO:	Think carefully Whether, by other means—
ROSAURA:	—To be destroyed In some other way!
CLOTALDO:	If you are bent On self-destruction, My daughter, wait Wait, and let us Face ruin together!

The Battlefield.
SEGISMUNDO, dressed in skins; SOLDIERS, *marching*. PIPER.
Drums are heard.

SEGISMUNDO: If Rome's ancient pride
           Could see me now today in triumph ride,
           She would behold amazed
           Her mighty armies captained by a mountain
              beast
           Before whose high ambition
           Small seems the conquest of Jove's heaven!
           But, soul of mine,
           Our soaring aspiration let us now restrain,
           Let us not take pleasure
           In this uncertain glory beyond measure,
           For when I wake
           Greater the loss, if I should too much pleasure
              take.
           The less we set our love
           Upon such things, the less their loss can
              grieve.
PIPER: On a swift stallion—
           Excuse me, but I must take this opportunity
              to discourse
           Upon the horse in question—
           For he is a perfect model of the universe
           In his own person.
           His chest is a furnace, ocean foams at his
              mouth,
           His body is earth,
           The wind his breath—earth, air, fire, water,
           An elemental monster!
           He is approaching chaos, a mixture

Fourfold of spirit, breath, body and froth—
A dapple gray,
Becoming dapple red, thanks to the tender
    mercy
Of one who comes riding
Clapping spurs to his sides, not galloping but
    flying—
    O there has ridden o'er field and fell
    A lovely maid to thee!

SEGISMUNDO: Her beauty blinds me!
PIPER: Your Highness, it is Rosaura. (*exits*)
SEGISMUNDO: Heaven once again has brought her!
ROSAURA: Generous Segismundo,
You who are emerging
From your night of shadow
Into your day of greatness,
As the great sun rises
In the arms of morning
And to the rose brings colour,
To the verdure brightness,
Bathes the mountain summits
And gleams upon the waters,
So may your rising be,
Glorious sun of Poland!
An unhappy woman
Begs for your protection,
Kneeling at your feet—
Unhappy, and a woman—
Each of these alone
Should awaken pity
In a man of honour.
Three times you have seen me:
For three times I have come
In a new disguise.
First you saw me as a man,

98

When, in a dark prison,
Your griefs comforted mine;
Then, the second time,
As a woman you admired me,
When all your majesty
Vanished like a dream,
A shadow, or a phantom.
This is the third time:
Now, both man and woman,
—By my dress a woman,
By my arms, a man.
Now you shall hear the story
Of my life's tragedy,
And surely your compassion
Will incline you to protect me.
I come from Muscovy,
Child of a noble mother,
A lady, whose great beauty
Is matched by her misfortune,
For a villain, of whose name
I am ignorant,
Cast his eyes upon her.
I say, I do not know
His name, but of his daring
I can testify, by mine;
And since I am his daughter,
I wish I were a pagan,
For then I could believe
My father was the god
Who in metamorphosis
Came as a shower of gold
To Danae, the swan
Of Leda, or the bull
Who bore away Europa:
All tales of perfidy—

For, like these, my mother,
Matchless in her beauty,
Was deceived by words of love,
And, like these, deserted.

So deeply did she trust
His faith, and vows of marriage,
That even now she weeps
When she remembers him;
But he, like false Aeneas
Of Troy, left her a sword.
Now the blade is sheathed,
But it shall be drawn
Before my tale is ended.
So of this ill-knit bond
That neither binds nor holds,
A marriage, or a sin,
(Though both are much alike)
I was born, so like my mother
That I became her copy
Not, indeed, in beauty,
But in actions and misfortune.
What more shall I say?
I am my mother's daughter,
My story is like hers.
One thing more I must tell you
About myself—the man
Who brought me to dishonour
Is Astolfo—when I name him,
My enemy, rage and shame
Fill my heart! Astolfo
My ungrateful victor
Soon forgot his conquest—
For the memory
Of past love is soon forgotten—

And he came to Poland,
Summonded by ambition
To a more illustrious triumph,
To pay court to Estrella.

Estrella was the torch
Of my setting sun!
To think that all the stars
Combine to bring together
Two lovers, yet one star,
Estrella, can divide them!
Outraged and deceived,
Sad, mad, dead with grief,
I was left alone
With all hell's clamouring voices
In my living Babel.
I did not speak one word;
But there are sufferings
More eloquent in silence—
I told of what I suffered
Without the help of words
Till one day Violante,
My mother, made me speak.
I poured out all my sorrows
Without reserve—I knew
My weakness had been hers,
And in that thought found comfort.
Bad example may be helpful
At such moments. Well, she listened
With compassion to my woes
And tried to comfort me
By telling me her own.
When the judge has sinned
He cannot but be lenient!
She knew from experience

That time affords no cure
For the loss of honour.
She gave me her advice:
To follow my false lover
And compel him to fulfil
The debt he owed my honour.
To run less risk, I wore
A man's clothes, and my mother;
Took down an old sword
That hung upon the wall—
The sword that I am wearing—
And now the time has come
To draw the blade—for so
My mother made me promise.
'Go', she said, 'to Poland,
'Let the highest and the greatest
'At the Court, see
'The weapon; it may be
'That among them one
'May shelter and defend you.'
So I came to Poland—
I will hurry through the rest—
The horse that I was riding
Bolted in these mountains,
And by that mischance
I came upon your dungeon,
Where you were so astonished
To see me; and there, too,
I first saw Clotaldo.
He became my protector,
Pleaded for my life
To the King, and I was pardoned.
When Clotaldo heard my story
He persuaded me to wear
These women's clothes, and enter

The service of Estrella;
This gave me the occasion
To hinder Astolfo's courtship
And his marriage to Estrella.
I am in your presence
A third time, to confuse you
Once more, half man, half woman.
But to go back to Clotaldo:
Convinced that now Astolfo
And Estrella will be married
And reign, he has advised me
To sacrifice my honour
And lay aside my claim:
But on this day I see
That you embody vengeance,
For Heaven desires to free you
From the savage prison
Where you have been living,
A beast to human feeling
And a rock to suffering.
Today you take up arms
Against your country and your father,
And I come to your aid,
Robed like proud Diana
But armed like warring Pallas.
Therefore, dauntless leader,
Since you and I are eager
To prevent and break
The concerted wedding,
I, to prevent the marriage
Of the man who is my husband,
You, because, united,
They bring double force and power
To impede your conquest.
As a woman, here I beg you

To defend and help me,
And as a man I come
To urge you on to conquest!
As a woman, beg for pity,
As a man, to serve you come,
With my sword—but let me warn you
If you make love to me
As a woman, as a man
I will kill you in defence
Of my honour; in the conquest
Of my good name, as a woman
I plead, but as a man
I will defend my honour!

SEGISMUNDO: Heaven, if I am dreaming, suspend my memory!

How can so much be contained in a single dream?

Oh God, who could escape these things, or pass them by unheeded?

Into what doubt am I thrown! For if I dreamed that greatness

In which I beheld myself, how can this woman

Recount it all, just as it was? So it was real,

It was not a dream! But if real, no less strange;

For it seems I cannot distinguish the real from the dream.

Is all glory so like a dream that the real seems illusion

And the illusion, true? So like the shadow

The substance, that the substance seems the shade?

Is there so little difference, then, between waking and sleeping?

The copy so like the original we cannot tell which is the real

And which the replica? If that be so—
If greatness, power, kingship, like shadows
    fade,
Let us enjoy our span, for the only happiness
We enjoy is that of dreams!
Rosaura is in my power; my soul worships
    her beauty;
Why should I not capture this moment, let
    love break all the laws
Of chivalry, of the trust she places in me!
My soul, let us dream our pleasures
Now, for soon, it is sure, we shall dream of
    sorrows!
But my reasoning turns against me: for if this
    world is a dream
Who for its vain glory would forfeit the
    divine?
Is not all past happiness a dream?
Who ever enjoyed great fortune who did not
    later say
'It vanished like a dream'?
Disillusion, again! For if pleasure is only a
    dancing flame
Blown out by the wind and leaving nothing
    but ashes,
Let me seek the eternal everlasting glory,
Unsleeping joy, unwearied greatness!
Rosaura is without honour: it befits a
    Prince
To bestow honour, not to destroy it. Her
    honour I will win
Before I win my crown.
But now I must avoid this too strong temp-
    tation.
(*to a* SOLDIER)

	Call to arms! Before night's shadows drown
	the golden day
	In green-black waves, I will give battle!
ROSAURA:	Sire! Will you leave me
	Like this? Does my distress
	Deserve not a single word?
	Is it possible, my Lord,
	That you neither heed nor listen,
	Nor even look at me?
SEGISMUNDO:	Rosaura, I am bound
	In honour to defend you,
	Therefore I must be cruel.
	I must not speak to you
	But my honour will.
	I must not speak, because
	My actions must speak for me,
	Nor look at you, for he
	Who defends your honour
	Must not behold your beauty.

(*Exit with* SOLDIERS)

ROSAURA:	What does he mean? Alas,
	After so many sorrows
	I meet only fresh doubts
	And strange ambiguous answers.

PIPER: May I say a word to you now, Madam?

ROSAURA: Piper? Is it you? Where have you been?

PIPER: Shut up in a tower playing at cards with death
           With my life on the stakes.
           He and I dealt in turn.
           One more hand and he would have won the
               jackpot
           I was *in extremis!*

ROSAURA: But why?

PIPER: Because I know secrets!
           I know who you are—yes, and that Clotaldo
               is—
           What's that noise?

ROSAURA: What can it be?

PIPER: The Royal cavalry! They have set out—
               they're coming
           This way—they are engaging now with
               Segismundo—

ROSAURA: As a coward I shall be shamed before all the
               world
           If I am not found fighting at his side
           When lawless cruelty is loosed. (*exit*)

VOICES: Long live our noble King!
OTHERS: Long live Liberty!
PIPER: Long live liberty *and* King, say I,
              Live and let live; what do I care?
              The war is no concern of mine.
              I'll play Nero and let Rome burn!
              But my own skin's another matter—
              I'll hide here, and watch the fun.
              Among these rocks I'm out of danger—
              Death can never find me here,
              So a fig for death, I say!
                    (*hides*)

Scene Eleven

Enter BASILIO, CLOTALDO *and* ASTOLFO, *in flight.*

BASILIO: Never was King so unfortunate!
                Never was father so pursued!

CLOTALDO: Your army is retreating in disorder.

ASTOLFO: The traitors are victorious!

BASILIO: In all such wars as these
                Victors are always loyal,
                And the vanquished always traitors.
                Clotaldo, we must flee
                From the cruel unnatural fury
                Of my tyrant son!

(*A shot is fired, off, and* PIPER *falls down from his hiding-place*)

PIPER: God have mercy!

ASTOLFO: Who is this poor soldier
                Fallen bleeding at our feet?

PIPER: I am a poor luckless fellow
                Who tried to hide from death, and he
                Found me here; I ran away
                Straight into his arms! No-one can play
                Hide-and-seek with Old Mortality!
                The fastest runner finds him first.
                Take a dying man's advice,
                Go back to the thick of battle!
                It's safer among swords and bullets
                Than in this mountain hiding-place.
                No-one can run away from fate—
                If your name's on the bullet, it will find you!
                You think you will escape death if you run
                     away?
                But you will be running to your death
                If it is God's will that you should die!
                (*Dies*)

BASILIO:	You will be running to your death if it is God's will
	That you should die! How well,
	You heavens, this poor corpse teaches us
	Our error, shows us our ignorance!
	It speaks through a wound's mouth,
	Its humour is uttered by a tongue of blood,
	Telling how vain are man's endeavours.
	To strive against the greater force, the primal cause—
	As I have done! I tried to save my kingdom
	From bloodshed and civil war, only to deliver it
	To those against whom I pretended to protect it.
CLOTALDO:	Sire, even though Fate knows all the roads
	And finds the man she seeks among the rocks and thickets,
	You must not, as a Christian, believe that there is no remedy
	Against its fury; there is,
	Indeed there is—for the wise man transcends
	His destiny, and if you are not immune from grief and misfortune
	You have the remedy in yourself.
ASTOLFO:	Sire, Lord Clotaldo
	Speaks with an old man's wisdom,
	I for the brave and young.
	Hidden in that thicket
	A horse stands ready tethered,
	A horse sired by the wind!
	Mount it and ride away—
	I will cover your retreat.

BASILIO: No, Astolfo, no.
             If God wills my death
             Now, and in this place,
             In this place I will stay
             And meet death face to face.

SEGISMUNDO: Somewhere among these bushes and rocks
the King is hiding.

Follow him—

Look behind every trunk, and among the
branches!

CLOTALDO: Flee, Sire!

BASILIO: Why so?

ASTOLFO: What are you going to do?

BASILIO: To do, Clotaldo? What I have to do!

Prince, you are looking for me, I believe—

Here I am. (*kneeling*) Let my white hairs be
your carpet,

Set your foot on my neck, trample my crown,
My dignity pull down,

Humble to the dust my self-esteem, take
vengeance upon my honour.

After all my strivings to avert this hour

Let Fate fulfil its law, Heaven's word be kept!

I am your prisoner.

SEGISMUNDO: Illustrious court of Poland,

You who have witnessed such momentous
deeds, attend!

It is your Prince who speaks.

What is determined, and by God's hand is
written

In numbers and figures of gold in the blue
pages of the skies,

Will come to pass; Heaven never deceives,
nor lies.

He only lies and deceives who deciphers and
interprets

Only to misunderstand the signature of
Heaven.

112

My father, whom you see, to avert the evil in
    my nature
Turned me into a brute, a savage;
For if—and from my noble birth it may be
    so—
I had been born gentle and docile
He by the upbringing he chose for me would
    have made me into a brute.
Was that a way to curb my faults, and form
    my character?
If a man is told, 'This savage beast will kill
    you.'
Will he then set about waking it from its
    sleep?
Or 'The sword in your scabbard will be the
    cause of your death.'
Will he draw it, and point it at his heart?
Or told that a gulph of the sea will be his
    silver monument,
Who would set sail when a storm is blowing
    the glassy waves
Into mountains of curling foam and blizzard
    of spindrift?
Yet this my father did: he has acted like the
    man
Who awakens the sleeping beast, draws the
    sword from its sheath,
And challenges the storm. Now hear what I
    have to say:
Suppose me a sleeping beast, my fury a keen
    sword, my rage a tempest,
None can conquer evil by injustice and
    cruelty:
Rather you arouse it; he who hopes to master
    his fate

Should act with temperance and prudence;
Only when the evil is upon us can we defend
ourselves;
For whatever means we choose for our
protection,
These are of use only when the occasion is
upon us.
May this unexampled, fabulous event,
This portent, this monstrosity stand as a
warning! Here you see my father,
After so many precautions, prostrate at my
feet, a King deposed.
This was Heaven's sentence; and if he with
the wisdom of age could not avert it,
Could I, less wise than he, less virtuous, and
without grey hairs?
Rise, Sire—give me your hands;
Heaven has proved to you how wrong were
the ways
You took for your revenge; I submit to your
judgement.

BASILIO: My son, by this noble act, you are reborn,
In my heart, as my own son; you are the
victor,
May your deeds be your crown.

ALL: Long live Segismundo, etc.

SEGISMUNDO: Yes, I intend to win
Famous victories!
And so, today, I aim
At the highest triumph,
That over myself!
Astolfo, give your hand
To Rosaura, for you owe her
A debt of honour, and I
Must see that it is paid!

ASTOLFO: But although it may be true
I am in her debt, remember
That she does not know her father
My dignity would suffer were I to marry
A woman who—

CLOTALDO: Stop! Enough, Astolfo! She is as noble as
you,
And my sword will defend her in any field.
Rosaura is my daughter.

ASTOLFO: What
Do you mean?

CLOTALDO: I did not intend
This secret to be known until I could see her
married,
Noble and honoured. It is a long story—
But what matters is—I am her father!

ASTOLFO: If that is so, I will fulfil my promise to her.

SEGISMUNDO: Nor do I wish Estrella
To suffer disappointment
And lose a noble husband.
I myself will see
That she too weds a Prince
Who, in respect of fortune
May not excel Astolfo,
But at least shall be his equal.
Will you give me your hand?

ESTRELLA: So I shall not lose
But gain much happiness!

SEGISMUNDO: And you, Clotaldo, who so loyally served my
father,
Come to my arms! For I am waiting
To give you anything you ask for.

1ST SOLDIER: If this is how you repay
Those who did you no service,
What will you do for me?

	I led the rebellion
	That freed you from your tower.
SEGISMUNDO:	Your reward shall be the tower; and to ensure
	That you shall never leave it until you die
	You shall be well guarded; who needs the traitor
	Once the treason is done?
BASILIO:	I applaud your wisdom.
ASTOLFO:	How he has changed!
ROSAURA:	Such prudence and discretion—
SEGISMUNDO	Why this astonishment and admiration?
	From a dream I learned a lesson
	And in my heart there is a fear
	That suddenly I may awaken
	And find myself a prisoner
	Walled once more inside a tower.
	That indeed may never happen,
	But what if I dream that it is so?
	From a dream I came to know
	That joy must vanish like a dream.
	And now, before my dream is broken
	I desire to use it well.
	The forgiving heart is noble,
	So may our sins be all forgiven!